MAYA LIN

ARTIST-ARCHITECT
OF LIGHT AND LINES

Designer of the Vietnam Veterans Memorial

JEANNE WALKER HARVEY • *illustrated by* DOW PHUMIRUK

Christy Ottaviano Books
Henry Holt and Company
New York

In loving memory of my parents,
June and Joseph Walker —J. W. H.

For Christy and Deborah,
who took a chance on me —D. P.

Henry Holt and Company, *Publishers since 1866*
175 Fifth Avenue, New York, New York 10010 • mackids.com

Henry Holt® is a registered trademark of Macmillan Publishing Group, LLC.
Text copyright © 2017 by Jeanne Walker Harvey
Illustrations copyright © 2017 by Dow Phumiruk
All rights reserved.

Library of Congress Cataloging-in-Publication Data
Names: Harvey, Jeanne Walker, author. | Phumiruk, Dow, illustrator.
Title: Maya Lin : artist-architect of light and lines / by Jeanne Walker Harvey ; illustrated by Dow Phumiruk.
Description: First edition. | New York : Henry Holt and Company, 2017.
Identifiers: LCCN 2016034687 | ISBN 9781250112491 (hardback)
Subjects: LCSH: Lin, Maya Ying—Juvenile literature. | Architects—United States—Biography—Juvenile
    literature. | Chinese American architects—Biography—Juvenile literature. | Artists—United States—
    Biography—Juvenile literature. | Chinese American artists—Biography—Juvenile literature. | Vietnam
    Veterans Memorial (Washington, D.C.)—Juvenile literature. | BISAC: JUVENILE NONFICTION /
    Biography & Autobiography / Women. | JUVENILE NONFICTION / History / United States /
    20th Century. | JUVENILE NONFICTION / Biography & Autobiography / Art.
Classification: LCC NA737.L48 H38 2017 | DDC 720.92 [B]—dc23
LC record available at https://lccn.loc.gov/2016034687

Our books may be purchased in bulk for promotional,
educational, or business use. Please contact your local
bookseller or the Macmillan Corporate and Premium
Sales Department at (800) 221-7945 ext. 5442 or
by e-mail at MacmillanSpecialMarkets@macmillan.com.

First edition—2017 / Designed by Eileen Savage
The art for this book was created digitally in Adobe
Photoshop with scans of watercolors and textures.
Printed in China by RR Donnelley Asia Printing
Solutions Ltd., Dongguan City, Guangdong Province

10 9 8 7 6

In the woods by her childhood home,
Maya Lin played with her brother
and explored and climbed the many rolling hills,
one she named the Lizard's Back.

On long walks alone,
she searched for birds in the forest.
Maya sat still as a statue,
hoping to tame rabbits, raccoons,
chipmunks, and squirrels.

In her house full of light
and open spaces,
Maya read books and
played chess with her brother.

And with paper and scraps,
she built tiny towns.

Her parents had fled China
at a time when people were told
what to be and how to think.
Her parents never told Maya
what to be or how to think.

Maya grew up with art.
Her father was an artist
who made art with clay.

Her mother was a poet
who made art with words.

She watched her father
form a pot from a mound of clay
without plans or drawings.
Maya, too, thought with her hands
as well as her mind.

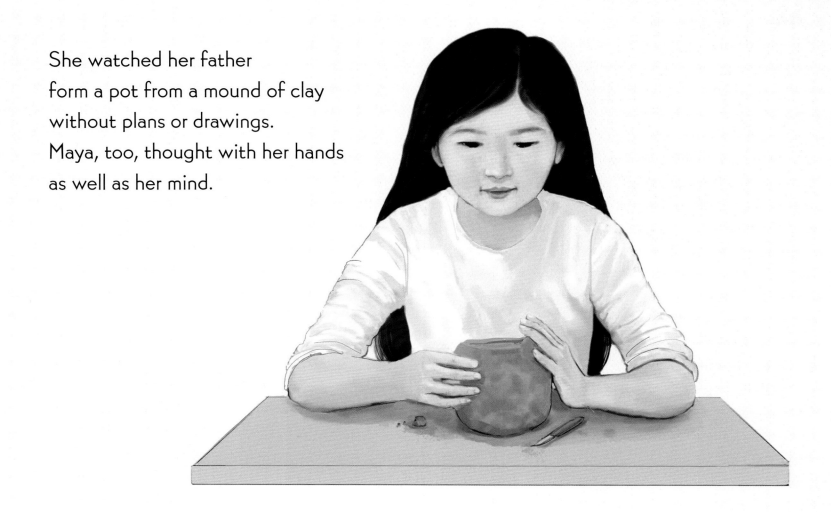

clay   ceramics   silversmithing   macramé

Maya graduated
co-valedictorian of
her high school class.

One day when Maya looked
at the patterns of light and lines
on the ceiling of her college library,
she imagined she would become an architect
who created buildings with art, science, and math.

While studying overseas,
Maya wandered through countries and cities
gazing at buildings of all types,

new and old,

learning all she could.

In her last year of college,
Maya entered a contest to design
a memorial to honor soldiers who died
during the Vietnam War.

The contest rules said the memorial
must blend with a park setting
and include the name of every soldier
who died fighting or was missing.
Almost 58,000 names.

These rules rang true to Maya.
She knew the power of names.
Maya believed that a name
brings back all the memories of a person,
more than a photo of a moment in time.

Back at school, Maya sculpted a model
with mashed potatoes, then with clay.

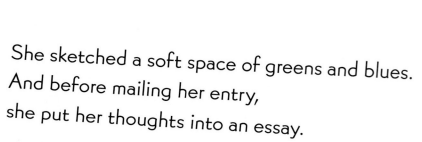

She sketched a soft space of greens and blues.
And before mailing her entry,
she put her thoughts into an essay.

She wrote that her long, polished wall would be a quiet place to remember all those who died during the war.

A place to be experienced
by walking down, then up past names that seemed to go on forever.

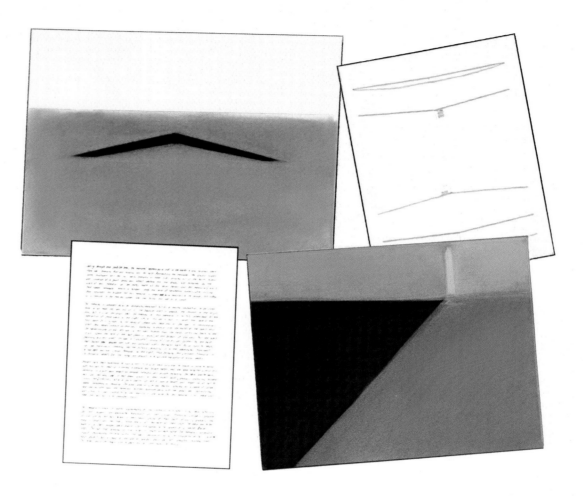

The contest received so many entries,
enough to fill an airplane hangar.
Lots of famous architects
and artists entered.
The names of the contestants
were hidden from view.

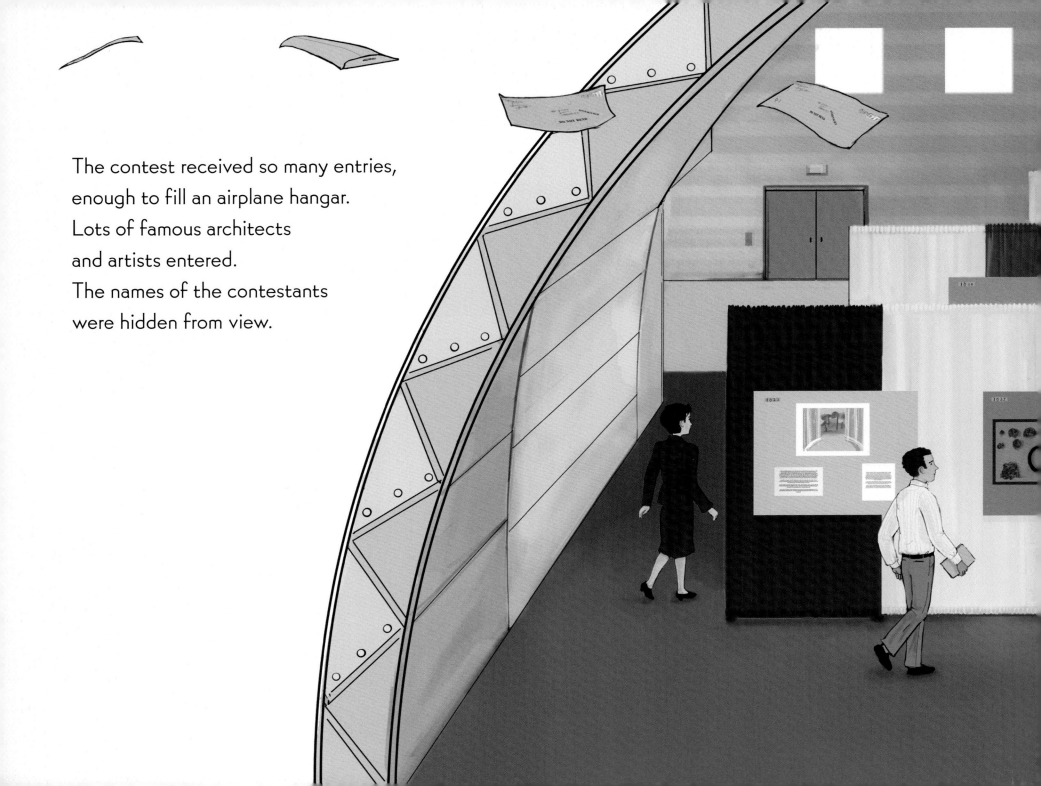

MAYA LIN!

Out of 1,421 entries, Maya's design was chosen.
Simple yet strong. Creative and new.
But when they found out Maya was the winner,
the judges were shocked. She wasn't famous.
She was a young woman still in school.

Maya was as surprised as the judges.
All was excitement, at first.
But then people objected.
Some said her design looked like a bat,
a boomerang, a black gash of shame.

Their angry words stung Maya.
For months, public hearings were held.
Some people wanted to change the design.
Maya was young, but she was brave.
She didn't back down.

Finally her design was approved.
Maya worked with a team
of architects and engineers
who devised plans
to excavate the land, build the wall.

The granite was cut, polished,
and engraved with the soldiers' names.
The earth was dug up.
Maya watched the panels,
suspended in space, set in place.

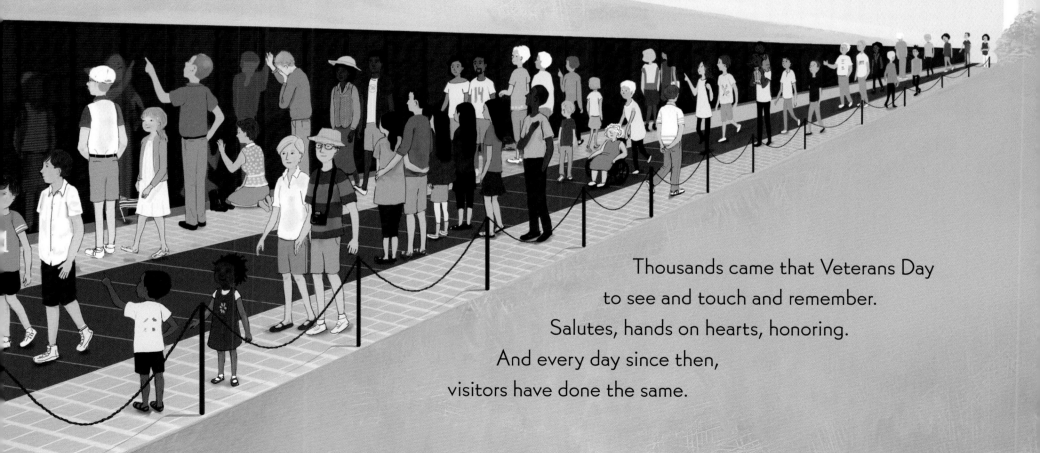

The first time Maya visited
the finished wall, she searched
for the name of the father of a friend.
When she touched the name, she cried,
just as she knew others would.

Thousands came that Veterans Day
to see and touch and remember.
Salutes, hands on hearts, honoring.
And every day since then,
visitors have done the same.

Sounding Stones

The Vietnam Veterans Memorial
was the first of Maya's many works
of art and architecture—
memorials, sculptures,
structures and spaces, inside and out.

Each piece is different,
but all share Maya's vision.
She wants people to be
a part of her art. Look. Touch. Read.
Walk around. Sit by. Think about.

Topo

The Wave Field

10 Degrees North

And just like when she was a child
who named a hill the Lizard's Back,
Maya names her projects, often words from nature.
Names such as Sounding Stones, Topo,
The Wave Field, 10 Degrees North, Reading a Garden.

Reading a Garden

And after naming a piece—
the final step in shaping her artwork—
Maya Lin, the artist-architect,
is ready to dream, think again,
and create something new.

paintbrushes

paint tubes

colored pencils

mixing tray

watercolors

clipboard

sponge

sketchbooks

ink pens

favorite pencil

pastels

doll

blueprints

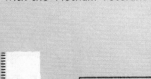
stencil

compass

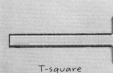
notebook

T-square

triangle

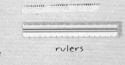
rulers

carving tools

clay

erasers

sharpener

pencils

paper

Author's Note

When I was a senior in college in 1981, I was thrilled to learn that another senior in college, the twenty-one-year-old Maya Lin at Yale University, had won the national contest with her stunning design for the Vietnam Veterans Memorial in Washington, D.C. I closely followed the news of the governmental hearings and challenges to her simple yet powerful design.

Maya explained that the monument should not be about what people thought of the Vietnam War, a controversial conflict in which the United States backed South Vietnam against communist North Vietnam. Instead, she wanted the piece to be honest about the loss of lives in war and to honor the sacrifices of all who served.

The concept of time reflected by the physical placement of the names on the wall, and of the wall itself in Constitution Gardens on the National Mall, was an important aspect of Maya's design. She insisted that the names be listed not alphabetically but chronologically by casualty date or date deemed missing during the Vietnam War, from 1959 to 1975. The names begin in the middle of the memorial and loop back, creating a circle of time, or a sense of closure. And the tips of the wall point to the Lincoln Memorial and the Washington Monument to connect the Vietnam Veterans Memorial with the nation's past.

Famous throughout the world, Maya has authored books about her work and received many awards. In 2005, she was inducted into the National Women's Hall of Fame. In 2009, Maya was awarded the National Medal of Arts.

She views herself as an artist-architect and has designed numerous site-specific installations, buildings, memorials, and sculptures. As with the Vietnam Veterans Memorial, her Civil Rights Memorial and the

Women's Table reference strong historical and cultural issues. As a committed environmentalist, Maya focuses on projects that bring awareness to biodiversity and habitat loss.

Born on October 5, 1959, in Athens, Ohio, Maya grew up in that college town, where her parents were professors. Her older brother is a poet and professor. She currently lives in New York City with her husband, and they have two daughters.

To learn more about Maya Lin and the Vietnam Veterans Memorial, visit Maya's studio website, mayalin.com; vvmf.org/vietnam-memorial-wall-design; and thewall-usa.com/information.asp.

© Bettmann/Getty Images

Maya Lin holds a scale model of her design on May 6, 1981.

rendering

X-ACTO knives

3-D model to scale